Why You CAN'T Earn $1,000,000,000 In 20 Minutes!

Understanding & Protecting Yourself Against Internet Product Scams & Rip-offs

By
Kimberly Peters

Disclaimer

While every effort has been made to provide accurate and truthful information in this book, the reader must understand that the content in this book largely represents the opinions and viewpoints of the author and should not be used as a definitive basis for making life changing decisions. Instead, red the information in this book and use it to develop your own insights and opinions that you can use to become more knowledgeable and aware of advertising and marketing. The writers, distributors and producers of this publication assume no responsibility for the use or application of any or all parts of this book. The reader assumes all responsibility for all applications of the information of this book.

Contents

Introduction

Today it seems there are more ways to sell things to people than there ever has been before. Where it used to be that we were limited to buying what was being sold in our neighbor or town or what we saw on television, now we have the ability to purchase goods and services from all over the world.

Purchasing has become easier as well and this presents both advantages and disadvantages for consumers. While we used to have to drive from store to store to compare purchases, we can now compare 15 businesses in 15 minutes just using our mouse and computer screens. While this is faster, it also eliminates the time we had to think about purchases before we made them.

How many times have we thought something was a good deal or smart purchase only to give it more thought and come to the conclusion that it really wasn't such a good deal at all?

How many times have we thought about something and realized that we didn't really need it in the first place?

With the arrival of internet purchasing and sites focused on making purchasing faster and easier than it ever has been, we need to be able to make the right decisions quickly because very often we don't have the time to drive back to the store or wait for the store to open the next morning.

In fact, businesses of all shapes and sizes are adopting the "timeshare" approach to marketing where they tell you that you have to make a decision now rather than wait to think it over. This is not done by accident. This is done because it has shown that this approach gets more people to buy more products than allowing them to wait.

While it is also true that there is more consumer regulation today than there has been in the past, the sad fact is that it is not nearly enough. As soon as a new rule is put into place, efforts are started to circumvent or work around that rule.

In fact, sometimes new rules are obsolete even before they go into effect!

Though some of those people reading this book might find this next statement somewhat cynical, it is true none the less. Advertising today is designed for one purpose only and that is to separate you from your money. It is about making your product look as good as it can be especially when compared to the competition. While there is nothing wrong with that, the problem comes into play when people make up things about their products or make false claims in order to close more sales.

It is not possible to avoid these types of marketing efforts or be 100% sure 100% of the time that you are buying exactly what it appears you are buying. So since we cannot escape this behavior, we have to learn how to deal with it more effectively. That is precisely what the focus of this book is all about. How to protect yourself so that you make more good purchases and get victimized far less.

Make no mistake about it; there are a LOT of good products out there that are marketed responsibly and accurately.

But there are others that are not so it is in our best interests to learn how to make the right decisions when it comes to purchasing products. Especially products offered over the Internet.

I am confident that as you read through this book you will automatically think of examples that you have seen or heard that pertain to what we are talking about. You will remember a website that used certain strategies to grab your e-mail or the last time you were told that you only had 12 minutes to decide or the opportunity would be lost forever.

The first step is realizing things for what they really are. The second step is knowing what to do when you get in those situations and how to make the best decisions that are in your best interest. When you can accomplish that, you will find purchasing products much easier and safer.

It Starts with YOU!

The first thing we would like to talk about is more of an attitude or approach thing. By that we mean how you look at purchases and advertising and protecting your best interests. This is important because some people have a distorted view when it comes to who should protect whom.

While there are agencies like the Consumer Protection Agency and the Better Business Bureau, there is just one person in this world that can do the very best job in protecting you. That person is you!

It makes sense when you think about it because no one knows you better than you. No one knows what you need better than you and no one knows what's best for you better than you.

So the first line of defense when it comes to protecting you is for you to become aware of what it is that you are considering purchasing. Do not expect someone else, or some agency or company to protect you. They can help but you are ultimately responsible for your safety and protection.

What agencies like the Better Business Bureau and the various Consumer Agencies have that you don't is the ability to regulate, prosecute and hold people and companies accountable for their actions and what they present to the public. They can create rules and laws and guidelines and force people to adhere to them.

These agencies are important because no one individual can have the expertise and background to know everything about everything. For example, it is not reasonable to expect one person to know how to design a car safely or how every piece of equipment is designed or manufactured. We might know these things about some products but certainly not every product.

So in essence these companies and agencies are there to assist us in protecting ourselves and to provide the expertise and enforcement when it comes to following the law and properly representing their products and services. While this does not mean we can always believe what we hear and read and take it as gospel, it does mean there are limits to what people can write or say about their products.

This does not mean that everyone follows these guidelines or adheres to those rules, though. There will always be those people who will bend the truth to the breaking point or even blatantly disregard the truth and outright lie. This has been going on for centuries and it is not about to stop anytime soon.

So in order to protect our best interests we need to take control over our buying conditions and purchases and take responsibility for what we buy and where we buy it from. This is important because once we take responsibility for what we do; we take ownership of the consequences and outcome as well.

When we take responsibility we tell ourselves that we can have some control over what happens to us. We tell ourselves that we have to be on alert when it comes to how and where we spend our money. We tell ourselves to question everything before we make a commitment so that we protect our best interests.

When we expect others, or rely on others, to protect us, we give away some of the protection we would normally have if we were to protect ourselves. Another example might be that we can rely on the police to protect us from robberies or we can allow them to protect us while we look our doors and report suspicious behavior in the neighborhood.

In other words, the best way to protect ourselves is to use the tools and resources available to us IN ADDITION to our own efforts so that we make it far more difficult for people to rip us off or cheat us. When we focus our efforts on looking out for ourselves, we almost always get a higher level of protection than when we sit back and expect others to do the protecting for us.

The Internet Storefront

One of the most troublesome parts about purchasing online is not really knowing some of the businesses that we are considering purchasing from. When we purchase from a brick and mortar store in our neighborhood, we can walk into the store, touch and feel the products, and see for ourselves the type of business and people we are dealing with.

With Internet based businesses all we have to go by are the websites we see when we go to their web "address" or URL. From the website we cannot tell if this is a legitimate business with a storefront or warehouse and employees or some guy working out of his bedroom closet.

We also cannot see or touch or otherwise examine the products either. We cannot judge quality or size and we have no idea what the content is when it comes to printed material or information based products. So in many cases we are purchasing blind, basing our decisions only from the words we read and the pictures we see. All of this might be fine if the information and visuals we get are accurate and honest.

One of the most common issues occurs when we either don't receive a product we ordered, we receive a defective product or when the product we get is not what was described or represented on the website. In these cases, we need to either return the product for a replacement or a refund. This is where the fun can start.

If you purchase a product at your local store and you have a problem, you can take it back to that store and deal with an employee to get your refund or replacement. But when you purchase something online, you usually have to rely on e-mail or some support desk (located God-knows-where) to handle your complaint.

If the business is reputable and responds to your problem you will get your matter resolved. But if they don't answer your e-mails, and they don't respond to your support tickets, what do you do then? You cannot walk into the website and talk to a real live person. You cannot physically escalate the issue when things don't go the way you think they should.

Even more important sometimes is that when you purchase from an Internet company that is out of your state your local Consumer Affairs but not be an option. Instead you might have to contact the Consumer Affairs people in the state where the company is located. Sometimes you will have no idea where the company is located. In some cases the company might be located in another country altogether and that brings its own challenges.

There is another factor that most internet consumers never stop and think about. When you open a brick and mortar storefront, there is usually several hundred thousands of dollars involved in getting the building, purchasing inventory, hiring employees and other established costs.

This makes it difficult for someone running a scam to make a decent profit unless the scam is a very high level scam potentially worth millions to the scammer.

But it is so cheap to open an internet website almost anyone can do this for less than $50! In fact, you can purchase a domain name for less than $15 and use a free website builder and have a website up and running in less than a day or so and the whole thing won't cost you more than $25!!!!

Because of this scammers can put up a cheap website, steal or cheat a bunch of people and then just disappear. Or, they can just sell cheap or inferior products and stay in business until their reputation catches up with them and they close down the website and open the same business under another name.

Of course the great thing is that people like you or I that have access to a great idea or a great product can get into business for a low fee as well and this brings more great products to mass audiences. So not every website is a rip-off and not every new site is a scam. In fact, legitimate sites significantly outnumber scam sites. But the potential is out there.

Another factor which makes the internet so wonderful for scammers and cheats is the lack of personal interaction. It is one thing to cheat someone in person where the threat of retaliation or being exposed and something else entirely to hide behind a website and cheat people anonymously.

So the question should be "How can I protect myself when purchasing something on-line?"

Here are a few things you can do:

There should be a way for purchasers to contact the website to report problems. If there is no way to contact the website, then I would pass on purchasing from them.

Check to see if you are purchasing a brand name product. If you are purchasing a brand name product you might be able to get assistance through their warranty and not have to worry about the website where you purchased it. But even in these situations who is to say that what you see on the site is what you are going to get. They might advertise a brand name product and ship you something else.

Do a search under the company's name and see if there are a lot of complaints against it. A few is normal as some people complain about everything. In fact if you see a host of positive reviews and not a single neutral or negative review, that could be a warning sign. It might surprise some of you to know that scammers will put in phony reviews to convince people to purchase from them.

Check and see if the same product is available from a larger and better known place. Purchasing a product from a well-known and respected company should be safer because their reputation is important to them. They also got that reputation by treating people well. You don't get to be an internet giant by screwing people over!

If the product is available only from that one source, read the site carefully. Does the sales copy seem reasonable or is it fancy and full of high level promises and claims. If the sales pitch is over the top that should be a red flag for you.

Usually the lure of purchasing online is either because you have access to products you cannot get locally or because the prices are lower online. I would say if the savings are not considerable, I would purchase locally.

For example, if a TV is online for $499 and available locally for $509, if everything else is equal I would purchase it locally. If it was available locally and the lowest price was $699, then the risk might be worth the reward.

But to make things even less clear, if the price is really lower then you should ask yourself how they can sell something for that much less. Is the product what they say it is? Is it new or refurbished? There are no 100% tried and true methods of insuring you get what you paid for. But if you stick with established and known online stores you will likely have less trouble than you would if you bought from that guy working out of his bedroom closet.

Reviews Disguised
as Sales Pitches

Years ago, the internet used to be a place where you could get information to help you make a decision or learn how to do something you need to do for some reason or another. You could also search online about a specific product and get some real-life feedback and reviews from people who actually bought the product and used it.

This was great because you know you cannot take a salesman's word for anything because they are focused on closing a sale. But you could also go online, read some real-life reviews and find out the good and bad points of that particular product. It was good and unbiased information that you couldn't get anywhere else.

Then some jackass figured out a way to screw all that up.

Some genius decided it would be a great marketing ploy to disguise a sales pitch as a review. They would give a great review and go on and on about how great a product was and then include a link where you could go to purchase that product. But that link was an affiliate link which meant that the person writing this "review" would get a commission when the product was purchased.

Go out on a search engine right now and pick any product and do a search. Depending on the product you will find the first 2 or 3 pages of search results dedicated to these phony reviews. That is because the website and wording is designed to rank high on search engines so their page gets the most response or "hits".

So you don't get accurate information or learn the truth about something by searching for that product. But now I know what you are thinking. You are thinking that if you read bad reviews they must be accurate because no one would purchase a product from a bad review therefore no commission would be generated.

So the only reason someone would post a bad review was because they product really was bad.

Wrong.

Perhaps that same genius also figured out that you could also earn money by trashing products! You would write a review trashing a particular product but at the end give a link for a much better product. The person would then go to that link and buy the other product and generate a commission.

Another reason to post bad reviews is to also make your product look better by making another product, usually one of your competitor's products, look worse. You say their product can't do this and can't do that. You say it is over-priced or poorly made or any number of reasons and the result is the potential buyer is scared away. He or she might then turn to your product as an alternative. Of course you would also have a great review of your products.

People are also known for creating their own "reviews" of their own products and posting them on their sites as reviews or testimonials. This makes their products look great even though they might be the biggest pieces of crap on the internet!

Please understand that not every review or forum entry is a marketing effort and not a real review. They problem is that people go to great lengths to make their marketing or sales pitches look and read like real reviews so it is very hard to tell the difference between a real review and a phony one.

I always look at any link that is included in any review. If there is no link at all that is a good sign especially for a positive review. It still might be written by the person selling it but without a link at least it is not an affiliate offer for commission. If there is a link then I hover over it and look at the web address for that link. If it is a long link full of characters and numbers that is a clear sign of an affiliate link.

If the link provided is an Amazon link, that link generates a commission as well. It does not mean the "review" is false or misleading, it just means whoever wrote the review is gaining something by generating sales. So there is at least the potential for a conflict of interest in play with that review.

If you want to purchase something online that you are not sure of, make several searches and read the "reviews" with the information provided in this chapter in mind. This will enable you to at least identify the blatant sales pitches from the real reviews. Search several times and read several reviews and forum posts. You should be able to get a pretty good idea from all that you read.

A general rule of thumb is to investigate according to the price of the item. If the item is cheap and you have little to lose, just read a few reviews or articles. But if the item is expensive, read many more articles or reviews and summarize all of them in your mind before deciding whether or not to purchase.

The more information you gather the less you rely on any one or two pieces. You can then make a more informed and accurate decision because you have more information on which to base that decision that might otherwise go unnoticed.

Is this approach 100% effective? No, it isn't because people are always looking for ways to make the bogus review appear like the real one. But knowledge is power and knowledge can help you filter out some of the crap

Real Value vs. Perceived Value

One thing about value is that the real value of any product depends on the person using or purchasing that product. Something might be worth $10 to you but be worth $1,000 to me depending on the product and our needs at the time. So value can be relative.

On the internet many marketers use value and push it to the extremes in order to get you to purchase a product.

Bonuses are not a new thing by any means. They have been used for decades to increase the perceived value of a product. Infomercials on TV will "double your order" if you pay separate shipping and handling. Or the manufacturer will give you an accessory for the product for free if you purchase the product within the next 24 hours.

The variations are endless but the intent is the same.

One important thing to remember is that no marketer or manufacturer will deliberately understand or under value their product. It just wouldn't make sense for someone to try and sell you a product by telling you it is worth less or can do less than it really does. So if you see an advertisement, don't think for a minute that the product really is capable of doing much more than the description states because it is almost guaranteed not to be the case. The only exception might be if you figure out a new or different application that makes it worth more than its original application.

Sometimes, however, marketers and businesses will overstate the real value of their products in order to make them more impressive or desirable. So they tell you that the real price is $99.99 but for a limited time you can get it for $19.99. They want you to feel that this is an unbeatable off that you just have to grab right now.

The rule of thumb should be that no matter what the stated "regular price", the sales price, no matter how low, will still allow everyone to make a profit.

So that supposed $99.99 product that is selling at $19.99 costs much less than that $19.99. This is because the manufacturer makes a profit, the distributor makes a profit, the business selling it makes a profit and sometimes the selling person earns a commission. Though the actual cost will vary widely, that $99.99 product that is selling for $19.99 probably costs less than $7-$8 to make!

Sometimes the value of something has nothing to do with the cost of making the product.

An E-Book for example, costs almost nothing to deliver to a customer after the initial writing. Once the book is written and placed on sale the book is delivered digitally which means there are no shipping or handling charges involved so all the purchase price, less any commissions and a few cents for the bandwidth used to send you the book, go direct to the seller. In these cases it is not so much what it costs to make the book but rather the value of the information contained in that book that sets its value.

But this is where things really get crazy, or even funny, once you understand what the heck is going on with some digital products!

I had an offer come across my e-mail yesterday that featured a $27.00 E-Book on the subject of a certain aspect of internet marketing. The person selling the book had some bonuses if you purchased his or her book. Now usually a bonus is some fraction of the total selling price of the product. For example, you buy a blender for $99.00 and they give you an attachment for the blender that is worth $25.00.

But this person, or the affiliate selling the product, was offering a bonus package supposedly worth $6,795.00! So if I buy that $27 product, I would get **29 times** the purchase price of the product in bonuses! Wow! What a phenomenal deal! I mean, who wouldn't snap that deal up without even a second thought!

But before we whip out our credit card, let's take a look at this bonus package. This is usually good for a laugh. These bonuses usually consist of digital product that have little to no cost of sending you. This does not mean they have no value. It is just means they cost nothing to get into your hands.

But the stated value of some of these items appears to be very high if not laughable. Is that piece of software that is already 5 years old really for $495? Is that 6 year old e-book really worth $47? And that special training video where they teach you how to use the software, it that video really worth $497? Possibly but most probably not!

The point here is that a digital product is something where the stated value might have nothing to do with reality. I can write a book and decide what its "real value" is and set it at any value I want. Naturally the more valuable I make it appear in my sales copy the higher price I can charge for my book.

I have purchased many e-books and some of them were good while others were blatant rip-offs worth nowhere near their stated "value". My general rule of thumb is that if I get enough information or knowledge from a book to cover what I paid for it, then that purchase was OK. I bought one book once that was almost worthless but I picked up one little tidbit of information that helped me immensely when it came to properly marketing my products.

So even though the book was garbage, that one little bit of information made it worthwhile to me. Others might have felt totally ripped off.

It is up to the buyer to establish what any product is worth to them. I strongly urge you to take the sellers valuation and throw it out the window especially when it comes to internet marketing products or e-books. Don't even use it for comparison purposes because those stated values are almost worthless.

Don't make purchases because of so called "bonuses" either. If you like the product and they product appears to have value for you, then buy it and figure the bonuses are just that, bonuses. They will probably be worth a lot less than they say they are. After all, if I told you that I would give you $6,000 if you purchased a $27 product, wouldn't you think I was 100% drop dead crazy?

What I sometimes do if I get an e-mail with an offer for a product I find interesting is that I will first do a search for that product. Sometimes the search will uncover the same product for less money or at a discount. Other times I might find the same product at the same price but with more bonuses.

In that case, since I was going to purchase the product anyway, I might as well get the most from my money as possible. But again I stress that I do not purchase anything based on the stated value or over blown bonus packages.

The important thing here is to always figure out what something is worth to you not what someone tells you something is worth. As we said, I might find out a product solves a really critical need for me so the value to me might be through the roof. But for you the same product might be almost worthless because you don't have that specific problem. Both valuations are 100% accurate.

You just need to be aware on how to set your personal value on a product before you buy it.

Checking the URL

There are a lot of sites out there not so much to sell you something or provide information but instead steal your personal information or infect your computer. These sites use malware and other programs to infect your computer and help them access files without your knowledge.

In most cases the result will be a virus that changes the way your computer operates. It might change your internet browser home page, cause ads to pop up or force you to use a specific search engine designed to give you tainted search results. In some cases the computer may fail to start or operate at all.

But in other cases your personal identity, bank account numbers and other personal information might be at risk. Because of this, and the hassle and trouble this can lead to, it makes sense not invite these people into your computer or your world.

However, this is sometimes a lot easier said than done.

With this in mind, here are a few things you can do to not only protect your identity and your computer but to also protect yourself when you are looking at or purchasing something online:

First and foremost, get yourself a good anti-virus program. Make sure the program you use has the ability to scan e-mails as well. This way if you should get a virus trying to get into your computer through an unknown or seemingly innocent process, the anti-virus will stop it from installing itself. There are several programs out there and a few free ones such as AVG Anti-Virus that you can use. (We are not endorsing AVG or any program and no program will protect you 100% of the time!)

Second, install a mal-ware protection program on your computer as well. This program will search your computer for the programs that work in the background and reduce your security and effect the operation of your computer.

It is a great idea to run a scan on both your anti-virus and malware protection at least once a month. Once a week, or whenever you think something is not quite right, is better.

Third, NEVER click on a link that is enclosed in an e-mail that you are not familiar with. If some e-mail just appears in your inbox, delete it. But even if the e-mail appears legitimate, you still need to do a little checking.

Scam e-mails are designed to get you to share account information, passwords and other data. The scammers do their best to make these e-mails, and the sites the e-mails direct you to, look as professional as possible and extremely close, if not downright identical, to the real site. The idea is to get you to believe that you are really sharing information with your bank or financial institution when you are really giving it to scammers.

If you get an e-mail asking you to confirm your account numbers and/or passwords for whatever reason, do NOT click on the link and provide that information.

Instead, contact your financial institution directly using a phone number YOU HAVE. Do NOT use any phone number in the e-mail as this will take you to the scammers "call center" and they will portray themselves as your financial institution and ask you for your information.

If possible, go to the branch in person and ask if the request is legitimate. If it is, give your information to a person at the branch. If that is not possible, confirm the number you have for your financial institution by looking in the phone book, use older bank statements or other means to make certain you are calling the real financial institution and not a scammer.

Another tactic scammers and cheats use are URL's (web addresses) that appear at first glance to be legitimate but are instead just very close to the real address. For example, if your bank's website is

firstnationalbank.co

the scam address might be firstnattionalbank.com which is a misspelling of the real address.

The idea is for you to glance at the link and think it is legitimate because you didn't notice the misspelling.

So if you see a link like bankkofamerica.com or FEDEXX.com or anything like that, be especially careful and do not click on it. Misspellings on purpose are rarely correct when it comes to web addresses.

The link should also have the same web address as the company as well. If you bank with Goldtrust Financial and their website is goldtrustfinancial.com then if you get an e-mail claiming to come from them it should have come from the same address. If it didn't triple check to make sure this is legitimate. It is also possible that the bank hired a third party to contact all their customers on their behalf.

Naturally if the web link is going to some other web address or e-mail account entirely, that should send up a huge red flag. The general rule of thumb is that if you are going to click on a link you had better know where it has come from. If you get an e-mail sent to you from an unknown person or business, be skeptical.

Be Careful What You Download!

The same guy, or perhaps his brother, that decided to create phony reviews to disguise a sales pitch probably came up with this too. As if things weren't complicated enough, even the right products might cause you problems as well!

One of the ways people get viruses and malware on their computer is by downloading free products. Without knowing they click on a link to download a free program and then all sorts of other programs and files are downloaded at the same time. These programs might contain viruses or adware that places ads on your computer without your asking for them.

Some of the more popular free download sites will do this. They will send you a free program but make their money from being paid to download other peoples programs at the same time they are sending you the free program. Some of the most common added programs are search engine browser hijackers that change your search options and all kinds of games.

That is why it is so important to have an anti-virus and anti-malware program on your computer. When you are protected by these programs the download will be stopped and you will be notified of the presence of a potential bad program and you will be given the opportunity to abort the download before any damage has been done.

While I would like to say beware of any free offer or download because money has to be made from somewhere, there are a ton or sites that offer their products free through legitimate and virus free downloads. So you just have to be careful.

One thing I always do before downloading a free program is do a search under the program name plus the word "virus" or "malware".

Then see if any results come up where people have had these problems after downloading that particular product. This can give you an idea of what you might be up against should you decide to download as well.

Under no circumstance should you download a single file on any computer if you are not being protected by an anti-virus and anti-malware program. Make sure your protection is active and run a scan weekly or after you have completed a free download to make sure nothing else was downloaded at the same time.

If you own a windows computer you should also check the list of programs that are installed on your computer to see if there are any you do not recognize. Also check the date they were installed as well. You might be able to connect the installed date with the same date you did a download of a program or product. If something is there that definitely shouldn't be, then use the uninstaller to get rid of it.

Advertising

Before we get into product claims and sales copy and all that kind of stuff, let's take a step back a bit and talk about what advertising really is.

Advertising is the marketing of products to people in print, television and other media. Advertising can be in print form, electronic form for television and radio, audio spots, written media such as articles and e-mails and visual media. Visual media would include ways of placing images or messages I front of our eyes to get them seen and noticed.

Advertising has two main purposes and the primary purpose would depend on the type of product and the focus of the advertising campaign. But in broad terms, advertising is designed to either sell a product or get the product out in front of the people.

For example, advertising a sale would be advertising designed to sell a product to people. Using media to let people know about something such as a political event or something just designed to make people aware would be an example of advertising something to create awareness. Sometimes the two types combine when both goals are the focus of an advertising campaign.

For this book, we are going to concentrate on the advertising designed to separate you from your money. That means the advertising that is designed to sell products and create income for those who sell them. This is the most common form of advertising that we see in our day to day lives.

Advertising, when done openly and honestly, is not a bad thing. Without advertising we would never hear about most of the new products, or even existing products that might help make our lives better, easier or more rewarding and fun. In fact, the driving force behind advertising are those same driving forces.

People respond best to advertising that shows them how to make their lives better or easier. In addition to those two things, advertising tries to show you how a certain product accomplishes those things and how it does it better, faster or cheaper than anything else. You can take virtually any advertisement and all the claims will filter down into one of those groups. If your product can make life better or easier and does that faster and cheaper than anything else, you've got a real winner on your hands!

As we said advertising isn't in itself a bad thing. But when people corrupt the process and turn fact into fiction or fantasy that is where the trouble starts. Because competition is so fierce in the marketplace and because there are so many similar product competing for the same consumers, people often resort to less than honest methods of advertising.

As we discuss advertising related issues and a few other things in the coming pages, always remember that good advertising is designed to paint a picture in the consumers mind. It is not good enough to tell a consumer why your product is the best you have to create an image of the consumer using your product and experiencing the benefits.

The more vivid and detailed an image you create the more your customer will remember it and respond to it when it comes time to purchase.

So ad copy is written to impress people and to help form that image in your mind. Each word is carefully chosen to create the perfect mental image. That is why you will see so many descriptive words or strong images in an advertisement.

A detergent will not just get your clothes clean. It will get them sparkling clean. A new diet will not just help you lose weight. It will instead melt the fat away leaving you with a new trim and sexy body the opposite sex will fall in love with. A great steak will not just taste good. It will cut like butter and melt in your mouth.

Now I can honestly say I have used many detergents over the years and none produced clothes that came out of the washer and sparkled. They were clean but they didn't sparkle. I have also tried many diets but never had fat just melt off in a puddle somewhere and I don't think the opposite sex was any more impressed with me than they were before I lost the weight.

Last, but certainly not least, I am a steak lover but have never had a steak melt in my mouth or cut like butter. I've had some damned good steaks that were really tender but there was no melting in my mouth.

That is not to say that there was any harm in those descriptions. We understand that claims are going to be overstated and we have become conditioned to the everyday hype and over the top claims we see in advertising today.

It is when claims and hype get so bad that they are no longer stretching the truth but snapping the truth in a million pieces. We see diets that claim you can lose 20 pounds in a month or how anyone can easily earn $20,000 a month with little or no effort while sitting on a beach in Maui sipping a Mai Tai.

Injecting a Dose of Reality into Advertising

In order to protect ourselves we need to develop a filter that recognizes and filters out all the over the top crap. Call it a BS filter or whatever you want but everyone needs to have it. We need it because this type of advertising does something that regular advertising doesn't really do.

Bad advertising exploits weaknesses in people.

Bad advertising capitalizes on problems and weaknesses that some people are desperate to solve. People who will believe anything in the hopes of getting rid of a problem or situation that has turned their life upside down. The recipe for this kind of advertising is to take a common and sometimes serious problem and create a quick and easy solution for it.

Do you know who buys the majority of those "get rich quick" products or courses? People who have little or no money. They are so desperate to get money so they can get out of debt that they take what little money they have and buy these get rich quick books, videos and courses.

Do you know who buys most of the "miracle sure" books we see on a wide range of health related issues? People who suffer from those diseases or conditions that are desperate for a solution where none has existed for them in their lives. The same goes for miracle vitamin or drug cures and diets. People are looking for miracle cures and will spend a fortune on anything they feel just might be the answer for their problems.

Keep this in mind because if you run across an ad or commercial that concentrates on quick and easy solutions or cures for anything, condition yourself to be critical and skeptical. In other words, get used to applying your BS filter to make yourself aware of bad advertising. This is your first level of defense.

Try and separate your feelings from your judgment when it comes to advertising. Inject a bit of reality into things. Remember that dull and honest copy, while completely accurate, just doesn't sell? People do not respond to dull and accurate. They respond to fancy ad copy that creates that detailed image. But don't let your needs or problems influence or distort your views on what is legitimate and what is pure unadulterated BS.

Next we are going to discuss some specific parts of advertising that you need to become aware of so that you can see things for how they really are and not succumb to the tricks designed to get you to buy something you shouldn't buy and be disappointed in the end.

Quick & Easy

OK, I get the quick and easy drivers in advertising. Everyone wants to do something faster or make something easier. And most products do in fact accomplish those goals very nicely. But there are some things in life that are just not quick and easy no matter how you might try to make them so. If everything were quick and easy then there would be no problems in this world.

The first example would be all those get rich quick with no effort products. Think about this for a minute: If it really were possible for anyone to earn a 6 figure income with little or no work and no special skills, why hasn't government provided this valuable knowledge or system to everyone on welfare or below the poverty line so we can all be rich?

They don't do it because it just doesn't exist! Granted one or two people or perhaps a favored group of people might be successful but just because a few people were successful does not mean that you will experience the same results. If you look closely to the ad content, you will see a small print disclaimer that pretty much says "Don't expect the same results because you probably aren't going to get them no matter what you do." Well, it really doesn't say that but that's what the fancy words really mean anyway!

These products provide certain amounts or type of knowledge and it is what you do with this information or knowledge that sets people apart from one another when it comes to results. You cannot make any kind of blanket statement when it comes to results everyone can achieve because everyone is different and everyone will have different situations as well.

For example, let's say that there is a book that outlines a plan where you can make $10,000 a month selling a particular type of product.

So I buy it and someone else buys the same product at the same time. But he has access to a 100,000 name mailing list and I am just starting out.

Well he can start his system off with contacting his 100,000 contacts and of course if the product is popular he is going to sell a heck of a lot more than I will. He might achieve that $10,000 a month goal while I might struggle with $100 a month. There are so many variables involved that it is almost impossible to determine how much you actually will make instead of what they say you can make.

The lesson to be learned here is that you have to carefully evaluate claims and statements and inject your own brand of common sense and interpretation into things to arrive at an overall analysis of the risk. As I have already said I have purchased several products that have turned out to be garbage overall but have included one or two small things that helped me in other ways. So while the overall value was not as expected, I did receive enough value to make the purchase price at least a break even situation for me. It might not be quick and it might not be easy but with a low price there is also low risk.

This works well with inexpensive purchases. After all, if I spend $10 or $20 on an e-book, it doesn't take much information or content for me to get my money's worth. Just one idea or concept can make it worthwhile. But if I am purchasing a $495 marketing course from someone, there had better be a whole lot of information in that course for me to get my money's worth!

Features, Benefits and Price

We have already talked about established value and how a products value can be arbitrarily set by the owner or distributors of the product. We also discussed how the stated value can be very far away from what the real or true value actually is. In other words, something is not worth $495 just because the sales page says it is. But it might surprise you to find that the exact opposite is also true. In fact, low prices can also work against you when you try and determine whether or not a product is a legitimate one.

Let's use the marketing product that claims to give you the ability to earn $10,000 a month.

If I had a product or a system that actually could produce that much income for anyone without hard work or special experience, why on earth would I sell that to someone for $17???? If the product was truly that special and that value, I should be getting several hundred dollars for that product! Certainly not just $17!

Imagine a drug company coming up with a drug that cured all types of cancer. If they really had such a miracle drug and it did everything they claimed it would do, do you think they would charge people $17 for that cure! Hell no! They would get thousands of dollars and people would be lining up around the block ready and willing to buy it.

Value and price are intertwined. There is a direct connection between what something is worth and what the product will sell for. No one goes into business with the idea of selling their products for less than what they are worth. Everyone who goes into business wants to get the most money they can for every sale of their product. It's really just common sense.

Every time you see a commercial or a print ad ask yourself "Is the price of the product in line with what the product is supposed to be able to do?" If the price seems way too low for the features and benefits the product provides, that should send up a red flag in your head. If the price seems to match what the real value of the product seems to be, then go ahead and continue your investigation.

But if this appears to be an amazing once in a lifetime product and you can get it for just $17 then perhaps you should wonder why the seller is willing to let this amazing product go for such a low price. One reason just might be that the claims are overblown and the product just doesn't deliver what it promises.

I Just Want to Give Something Back Approach

Call me a cynic but whenever I hear that someone is supposedly giving away great products at ridiculously low costs because they are so grateful for their own success that they want to give something back, I just want to either barf or laugh. I want to laugh because they think that some people will actually buy that load of crap and I want to barf because some people really do believe this!

People sell products because they want to make money. They may truly want to share their good fortune and the things that worked for them but they are not giving this information away, they are packaging it like a product and selling it.

If they truly wanted to give something back they would give it away for free instead of charging for it!

But wait, they have an answer for that one as well.

You see, if they gave this valuable information away for free too many people would have access to it and most of them would never do anything with it because they had not invested their money in it. So the reasonable thing to do to insure that people are successful is to make them pay for it so they will actually use it.

So, they are doing you a favor by making you pay for something instead of providing it to you for free. That is so nice of them!

The fact is people price things at a certain level because that is where they feel their "sweet spot" is when it comes to sales at a certain price point. They feel that even though they might sell 1,000 copies at $37.00, they will sell 10,000 copies at $17. That means making $37,000 versus $170,000!!! If they knew they could sell 100,000 at $10 they would do that because that would make them $1,000,000!!!

Yes, there are people who honestly want to help people become successful. Some of these people earn a fortune helping others and there is no problem with that what so ever. But profits are the motive behind this. Creating, launching and marketing a product is not an easy thing to do. It requires time and effort and money to launch a new product. Even if the desire is to help people, the desire to make the most money doing so remains the primary driving force behind pricing.

I'm telling you this just because I want to help you. And I am telling you this for free!

Affiliates

One of the most common forms of marketing is Affiliate Marketing. Affiliate Marketing is where people pay others a commission or percentage of the selling price for marketing their products to others. Depending on the affiliates themselves this can be a very fast and easy way to get your products out in front of large numbers of people for a reasonable cost and at low risk.

Affiliate marketing is popular because the product owner only pays a commission when he makes a sale. He doesn't have to pay upfront for advertising and he really doesn't care how much is spent by others advertising his product because he only pays when a sale is made.

Think about affiliate marketing this way: If I told you every time you give me $50 sale I will give you $20, then you would be happy to earn a $20 commission for just referring a buyer without having to worry about handling the order, taking the payment and delivering the product. I would be happy because I made $30 even after I paid you your $20 commission. You would be happy selling 100 orders and I would be thrilled paying 100 commissions.

With affiliate marketing the affiliate takes most, if not all the risk, when he markets a product and invests his time and money into reaching the right people who are most likely to purchase your product. An affiliate might purchase traffic or an e-mail list but if no one buys they receive no commissions. So the focus for an affiliate is to find the right people and once they find them to do everything in their power to turn those people into buyers.

And that's where things can go wrong for both the customer and the owner of the product.

There is little to no control over what the affiliate rights in his ad copy or e-mails and how they represent the product. An affiliate can make up his or her own claims, descriptions and marketing presentation. The owner of the product may never become aware that their products are being misrepresented to the public until angry customers complain.

When it comes to affiliate marketing you can usually notice an affiliate lick by seeing a link something like this:

http://errdtm.hop.clickbank.net

Or when a link redirect is used the link might look something like this:

http://www.websitename.com/likes/p roductname

In this case the term "likes might be interchangeable with "recommends" or "endorses" or some similar term.

The entire reason for a re-direct is to mask an affiliate link and keep people from either knowing this is a commissioned link or masking the real address so people cannot go in and steal their commissions.

While there is nothing wrong with affiliate marketing, when I come in contact with what I suspect is an affiliate offer, I will do a separate search for the product to make sure the affiliate is properly representing the product. Many times the affiliate will direct their customer to the products real homepage which is good. But other times they will create their own homepage with over the top claims and false statements which is bad.

If the offer appears legitimate and it is something I am considering buying I will make an attempt to purchase through the link that was sent to me. After all the affiliate did reach out to me and incurred a cost for doing so. The affiliate making their commission does not cost me any money so there is little reason to deny them their commissions.

But if the affiliate site is a hyped up site full of overstated claims and fraudulent statement I will do a search and once I learn the truth and still want to purchase the product, I will purchase it from an honest site to reward them for properly and honestly representing the product.

But that's just me.

Passing the Smell Test

Here is something that usually works pretty well if we only just give it a chance. Most of us have a pretty good intuition about certain things. In other words, we just have a feeling that something isn't quite right about something. We might not know exactly what that might be; we just know it's there somewhere.

You know what I am talking about. We see the car ads with the sleazy car salesman talking a million miles an hour. We see the cologne ads where the man gets rejected and then when he puts on the new cologne supermodels are falling all over him. The most common example might be the gorgeous wafer thin super models on diet ads or endorsing products you just know they have never used and likely never will use.

Some of these things in ads are very obvious to most of us while some are designed so well that they sit there in full view but we just don't see them. Or, the most common thing is that the product promises to deliver such a powerful solution to our problems that we overlook our feelings because we hope so much that this is the answer to our prayers.

Intuition is a wonderful thing if we just pay attention to it. Our mind sometimes can't figure something out completely but it still recognizes that something isn't what it should be. When this happens we have two choices. We can pay attention and dig in a little deeper or we can ignore the feeling and move on. I say we dig a little deeper.

Whenever you read an ad or watch a commercial or video, pay attention. If you have questions or think something is not quite right, there usually is something either wrong or that we just don't understand in that ad or video. If that is the case we should stop and either educate ourselves about what we don't understand or stop and figure out what might be wrong.

There is a saying that goes "You can't put lipstick on a pig" which in our case would mean you can't make a horrible product into a great one. You might be able to make it appear better than it really is but in doing so you have to make claims that just do not ring true. In other words, you read or listen to the advertisement and your brain just knows it is reading BS.

Whenever I get that feeling the first thing I do is either watch the commercial again with a heightened sense of awareness or re-read the ad several times looking for other clues as to what's wrong. Sometimes the wording is done in such a way that a statement might appear to say one thing but legally say another. Or perhaps the content says you can expect one thing but the tiny print disclaimer at the bottom, placed there for legal reasons, says you likely won't experience anywhere near those results.

Usually I can find things "wrong" with the ad in that manner. If I don't, I start searching under that product to see if there are comments about that ad or product out there on forums and the search engines.

Reading a few of those comments or reviews usually adds a different viewpoint on things and also helps identify what was wrong or deceptive about that ad that bothered us in the first place.

Our intuition, or "sixth sense" is a powerful tool that we all need to use and pay attention to. If we can just turn off our emotions and remove the blinders we will see more of the deceptive nature of some advertisements and this will help us discover the really good ones while helping us identify the really bad ones. This is something we can all learn to do better over time if we would just try.

Sometimes the best way to protect yourself is to just pay attention to those little voices in your head that warn you whenever they think something is wrong. They help you avoid bad situation and will help you stay safe if you would just give them a chance.

If it Appears Too Good to Be True…..

There is an old saying that goes "If something appears too good to be true then it probably is. We should listen to that because way too often we just think something is the perfect solution and fail to recognize the obvious.

If I see a product that claims it will enable me to lose weight without diet, lifestyle change or exercise, I should be skeptical. After all, there is no medical reason for the body to lose weight if it does not consume fewer calories, burn more calories or make any changes whatsoever to how we live. That just doesn't make sense.

If there is a product that tells me that I can make one click of my mouse and earn $10,000 a month on auto-pilot without any work while investing no money and having no special skills or talents, that should set off a few warning flares as well.

But despite that these product often experience great sales because people dream about a life they wish they could have and often grasp at straws to get it.

Over the past few chapters we have discussed becoming more aware and separating emotions from the purchasing process. We should always ask ourselves "Does this product really make sense? Can it really do what it says it will do?" Even more important, we should ask ourselves probably the best question of them all: "If this product is so great and so easy why is it so cheap?" Or, in the case of those "get rich quick schemes: "If this method works so well and generates so much money, why on earth would someone share it with everyone?"

That is the great question when it comes to money making products or get rich schemes.

I am not saying that there are no new ways that help people make money. New methods and systems that really work do come about from time to time and they make people rich.

But those people who discover those new ways of earning money usually keep them to themselves or share them with just friends and family at first so they will be the only ones doing something and generating the most income. Only when those so-called "systems" stop working, or start to not work as well do they consider "sharing them with others".

Stop and think about that for a while. If you discovered a way to earn $10,000 a month would your first reaction be to tell everyone about it so they could do it and cut into your profits? Hell, NO! Your first reaction would be to continue making the money and keeping what you are doing a secret until you had enough money to choke a horse sitting in your bank account!

Even then, if you were sitting on a gold mine that actually delivered on your multi-million dollar promise, would you sell your wonderful idea on an affiliate network or would you share it with friends and family so that they could capitalize on your system as well? If you already made millions of dollars, why would you sell your perfect income generating gold-mine for $17 or $27 dollars?

Like we have said before, get rich quick products and "quick and easy products" target emotions in their advertising. They get us to believe that this product is the answer to our prayers. They try to get us to buy now, right now, before we have the chance to let the emotions go down and allow reality to set in. They need us to buy now because they know we will probably not buy later if given the opportunity to really think about things for a while.

Every day people who are desperate for one reason or another purchase products that promise great things. They do this not because they believe in the product but because they are desperate for a solution. They might have a serious health problem and are desperately looking for a cure. They might be in serious financial trouble and desperately searching for a way to earn a lot of money fast. Whatever the reasons, this is the emotional state that the sellers of these products want in their customers.

If something comes around that appears to be the answer to all your prayers or appears to be the perfect solution to a long standing and common problem, then watch out. These kinds of products, if they really were legitimate, would be worth millions or likely billions. They would be sold by reputable people and brand recognized companies and they would be expensive.

See things for what they really are and not what you need them to be. If you can do that, you will save yourself time and money as well as a lot of frustration and disappointment.

The Conspiracy Theory

Sometimes you see what appears to be a great solution to your problem and you wonder why this product is not being used by the general public. Maybe it's a diet that really works or a medical cure that is fast and easy and would help millions of people. This is a valid question and one that scammers and product marketers know they have to deal with. So they need to come up with a way to explain why your doctor hasn't told you about this amazing cure and why everyone isn't skinny because of their diet.

They have designed the conspiracy theory approach. The conspiracy theory works by convincing you that there are sinister forces in play that have banded together to keep this amazing product secret because it would cost industries a lot of money if this secret got out.

We have seen this many times over the year.

Decades ago when there was a gas crisis we heard of an amazing engine part that would get us 3 or 4 times the gas mileage we were currently getting. But the oil companies were refusing to allow this idea to get out to the public because they would sell so much less gas that their profits would plummet.

Then we have the miracle drug the doctors don't want released because people would take it, become cured and would not need to go to their doctors any more. Or, the pharmaceutical companies are banning the new miracle drug because it would make the other medications obsolete and cost them billions.

Now I am not for one minute saying that there are no conspiracies on one kind or another in this world.

In fact, I am fairly sure that there are a whole bunch of them going on at any given time. But I seriously doubt those conspiracies go so far as covering up new systems that generate extreme wealth or telling the public about how they can eat one special food that will cure cancer, diabetes, obesity and male pattern baldness!

Like other marketing tools, the conspiracy theory is designed to accomplish one thing. It is designed to mask the reason why this supposedly great product is not a mainstream and widely released product. It provides so-called answers to obvious questions that most normal people should be asking.

Most important, it is a theory that just cannot be easily disputed! After all, the nature of a conspiracy is that things are being kept from the public or held in secret someplace. So there is no way of people finding out the truth. If someone denies the conspiracy they will say of course they are denying it because of the money they would lose. In other words, they are lying.

So with one theory they provide a reason for the product not being well known and why it is not being manufactured or made available to the mainstream public. It is why their get rich quick book is not on the shelves of your local bookstore and why their miracle cure is not being prescribed by your doctor.

Remember when we said that a lot of advertising relies on desperation and solving of problems and emotions? Well, the conspiracy theory allows people to grasp on to one more reason why these products are the answers to their prayers. It gives them a reason to believe this product is real and that people in power are keeping it from them. In other words, it allows them to add more validity to the product in their minds.

This is not to say that any of these products is not what they say they are or that they do not work like they say they will. It is just that conspiracy theories and some of the other things we will talk about just should raise a few eyebrows and make you think that much harder about the rest of the advertisement.

Whenever you see the conspiracy theory approach used in an ad of any kind, your antenna should immediately go up and you should seriously investigate this product and products of similar kinds before making any purchase. Even low priced product with little financial risk could cause problems especially when the product is health related.

Check the product out. Talk to your doctor and really listen to what they have to say. Do your research and either confirm or disprove what is being said. There really may be a conspiracy in play here. But it just might be a conspiracy by a few people to separate you from your money as quickly as possible.

And that, my friends, is a conspiracy we can all do without.

Scarcity

Scarcity is another marketing tactic that many people use to get people to omit to purchasing now rather than later. There are two reasons people use this technique.

First, they do not want to give people too much time to think about purchasing. This is because the longer people have to think about something; the more likely they are to think about whether or not the claims and statements they are reading or watching are really true. If the product is not what it really says it is, the last thing they want to do is to have people really think about it!

Second, they do not want people searching all over on other websites to find out more about the product. There are two reasons for this as well.

The first reason is that they do not want people reading or seeing bad reviews or negative comments. This will help convince them not to make the purchase at all.

But the other reason is even more important. If you see the product on one site and then look around at other sites, there is a strong possibility that if you decide to buy you won't bother to go back to where you saw the product first. You either won't be bothered or you might not remember the web address of that site!

So the person who brought the product to your attention in the first place on that first site you visited will stand a very good chance of not getting their commission because you did not purchase it through their affiliate link! Lost commissions, depending on the product and the number of sales, could go into the hundreds or thousands of dollars!

So they create a scarcity perception by either limiting the number of copies available, limiting the time you can purchase the product, or escalating the price over time or by the number of sales made.

Any of these approaches creates a strong reason for someone to purchase now rather than later.

We have all seen limited time offers like store sales that are good for just one week or circular sales placed in our mailbox. But those are different as they do not imply limited quantities and they do not force you to make a decision right now.

The ads I am talking about are the ones that have a count-down clock on them telling you the offer will be gone forever in just a few hours. Or the ones where the price increases a few dollars or so after every sale is made. This is the same as telling the customer that they can still get the product tomorrow or the next day but they will likely pay much more for it. That pressures people into making quick, and sometimes bad, decisions.

Sometimes this is a scam and even though the offer has a 3 day time limit on it if you go back to the same webpage 3 weeks from now you can still purchase the product at the same price! But I have gone back to see if the products were still there and they were gone after those 3 days as well so you never know.

The scarcity ploy always struck me as being more than a little sleazy. I mean if your product is really good, and it really will help people make their lives easier or better, AND if you want to make money selling your product, why on earth would you put a time limit or a maximum number of copies limit on it?

Sometimes I get the max number of copies because sometimes you want to limit how many copies of something you sell so you do not over saturate the market and have too many people trying to do the same thing at the same time. That makes sense to me. But the other reasons appear to be there just to make people buy and buy now so people can either make money fast or, and far more likely, get you to buy without giving you the chance to really think about whether or not you should purchase.

One time Price vs.

A Subscription

Here is something I often struggle with because I can see both sides of the problem and both viewpoints as to which is better. While I'm afraid I don't have a definitive answer as yet, let's discuss this so you can be aware of both sides of this issue.

The issue I am talking about is whether subscription based products are better or more reliable than one time purchase products when it comes to delivering a quality product that performs as described.

For those of you who might not understand what I am referring to, let's say you want to learn how to market your products online and are looking for a product to show you how to do that. You find two good looking and sounding products.

The first product sells for $47 and looks great. The second product goes for $27 dollars a month until you cancel. So you pay more upfront for the one payment product but you probably will pay more for the monthly payment product because you probably will not get everything you need in the first month.

Here is the part that I struggle with at times:

I don't want to pay $27 a month for something when I don't know how long it is going to take me to learn everything, or most everything that I need to know about internet marketing. I also don't know how long I can expect to pay this $27 a month so I really don't know what the final cost of the product really is. But on the other side, if I pay $47 for a product that is a bunch of crap or doesn't give me what I need, I am out $47 instead of $27.

You see, common sense would dictate that the owner of the monthly fee product would have a huge incentive to keep providing fresh and informative content that has a value over that $27 a month because they want to keep people paying their $27 a month.

There are future profits involved here so the incentive is significant. The owner of the $47 product might not care because he already has the full payment for the product. To me this makes sense.

But on the flip side, the $47 product is likely going to have all the information about that topic or all the pieces to the puzzle it was designed to solve. So I would get all the information upfront to use as I see fit. But the subscription product owner does not want to give me everything upfront because I would just cancel after the first month. I mean, if you are not going to give me anything new why should I continue to pay my $27 a month? It seems to me that there is far too much pressure to parcel out the information gradually over several months in order to make more money and generate more profits.

For me personally, if the information I am being given is definitely worth more than the $27 a month, and the information continues to have that value each month or higher, I would continue to pay. I would pay because I was continuing to get the value of that information every month.

Plus, it is in the best interests of the product creator to keep high quality and informative information coming every month so that more people keep their subscriptions active.

I would say that before you purchase any subscription based product that you try to establish the value of the information you are purchasing. If the information is going to help you earn $10,000 then $27 a month is a pittance for that kind of information. But if the information is going to help you save $50, then I am not so sure I would pay $27 a month in order to save $50.

Product creators love the subscription model because it continues to generate income for them every month. But it will only do that as long as the creator keeps high quality information coming for his or her customers.

I would say this to those who are still undecided. If you are starting out with something and need to get started quickly or need to get an overall education on something new, you might consider starting out with a one-time payment product to see if that would be enough for you.

Then, as your business grows or your expertise increases, you can join a more involved or higher level subscription product to get the higher level information you may need to take your skills or performance up to the next level.

If you do decide to go with a subscription-based product, be aware that billing is usually automatic with automatic deductions from your PayPal or other account. This is important because if you forget about your purchase and do not check your account regularly, you could wind up paying for months of use you never even took advantage of!

My advice for anyone with a subscription based product is to write the renewal date at least one week earlier on a calendar so that you will have time to cancel as you are reminded each month. Doing this will help remind you to cancel if that is what you want so you won't be billed for services and information you never received or used.

It is both amusing and sad at the same time that marketers love products with monthly payments for this very reason.

They know that a certain percentage, much higher than you or I might believe, will forget about their purchase and keep paying month after month because they never check their account or read their statements!

The OTO

Here is another marketing ploy designed to make you part with even more of your money. Some of the time these One Time Offers are good and have a real value to them. But other times you buy a product that you expect to do what you need it to do based on the advertising and product claims and description only to find that the product you purchased has limited functionality.

Then you are told that for another payment you can "enhance" the product by unlocking new and special features. Usually the focus here is on quick and easy. By purchasing the upgrade the product will be easier, more powerful and get results even faster. Instead of telling you that they sold you a partial product, which they know would really aggravate you; they instead tell you that you should purchase an "upgrade".

Sometimes, if you purchase the first OTO you will be taken to a second, then a third or a fourth and so on. I would say the usual might be 2 one time offers but I have seen as many as 6 or 7 one time offer that you have to slog through in order to gain access to what you have already purchased. I can see one and maybe two, but the person who subjected me to those 6 or 7 I made a mental note never to buy from again.

I have no idea to being offered products or service that might possibly have value to me. For example, if I purchase a video creation product and the OTO is for video backgrounds or some audio tracks to use on my videos, I have no problem with that. But if I purchase a video creation product and then have to purchase 3 upgrades to make that program do what it was supposed to all along, I don't like that. Once I requested a refund without ever downloading the product because of all the OTO's and the stripped down product that I had initially purchased.

OTO's are a fact of life when you deal with downloaded products. You almost expect them. But you need to understand that OTO's are there because of you. They are there because the marketer realizes that you just bought one product so you are in the mindset of purchasing things online. Even more, you have already demonstrated your willingness to purchase from this merchant who means your advertising has created a certain level of comfort in their minds.

That means you are no longer a cold customer who has to be convinced to buy. You are already in the buying mood so they want you to continue to buy while you are in that mood. So they provide you with OTO's and they pressure you to purchase them.

I especially love what they make you click on to get access to your original purchase. You have to read and click on a link that says something like this:

"No, I am not interested in this special one-time offer. I realize that I am an idiot for doing so and will constantly kick myself for passing up on this no-brainer offer.

I understand that this offer will never be available to me again but I am so cheap and have so little desire to succeed that I will pass up on this wonderful offer forever and continue to be a loser for the rest of my natural life."

OK, it doesn't say exactly that in those words but the thought is the same. They want you to feel guilt for not purchasing. They want you to feel bad and perhaps rethink your decision. They use scarcity. They use guilt and they use pressure. When you know what to look for, you know how to deal with them.

If the OTO has value to you and is a valuable accessory or bonus, then you might wish to consider it. But if it adds more functionality to what now appears to be a bare-bones and stripped down product, you might want to abandon the entire thing and just demand a refund.

How to Save Money
on Many Online Products

Here is something that just might save you a few dollars when you finally decide to purchase an online product. It doesn't work for every product but it works for a lot of them and the savings could add up if you purchase several of these products a year.

These two strategies will cover the majority of your online purchases. They take just a minute or two but could wind up saving you a lot of money.

If you are purchasing a particular product, before you place the item in your shopping cart, open another window in your browser and enter in the search box the product name followed by the word "coupons".

If there are active coupons for a particular product they will come up in the listings and you would either use the listed coupon code or go to the site where the discount is listed and purchase through that link.

Now some of you might feel this is wrong because it might cheat the affiliate out of a commission but if you can find a lower price at another site, you should buy it there. If the affiliate expects to make sales they must expect people to want the best price or best overall deal. If they have no provided that, then the sale is up for grabs.

If you don't get any search listings try searching again and instead of the word "coupons" try the word "discounts" or "sale". You should come up with at least a few possibilities.

The second approach deals primarily affiliate products sold through websites such as ClickBank and similar sites. But they work on products sold directly by the creators as well.

If you find a product that you like and want to buy, before hitting the "add to cart" button or purchase button, make note of the website address and copy it. Then, exit out of the window. When you exit, many sites will see that you are leaving without buying and they will offer you a discount or other special deal in order to get the sale before you leave. I have saved at least $10 on each product I have purchased like this over the years. The site does this because they realize that a sale discount of $10 will mean less profit but still give them a profit. If you leave the site without purchasing they have earned nothing. So a little is better than nothing at all.

Now if no other offer is given and the window just closes or goes back to the home page, just take that web address that you just copied and open a new window and paste it in the address bar. This will take you right back to the original sales page so you can still purchase the product.

Copying the link is important because sometimes we reach a site through a few links and clicks and cannot find it again once we have left it. Taking 5 seconds to copy the link makes it easy to return if you should need to in the future.

The entire process should take you less than 2 or 3 minutes tops and can generate a nice savings on a lot of products. While $10 is not a huge amount of money it is better to have that $10 sitting in your pocket than to just give it to someone else and get nothing for it in return.

Sharing Your Experiences

I'm one of those people who hates to be cheated. Even if it is just for a few dollars, I don't like the fact that someone put something over on me and got me to agree to buy a worthless or over hyped product. I take it personally and it just bothers me. I also feel like I wished someone else had made me aware of this product or seller so I could have avoided the entire experience.

If I purchase a great product, I will write a favorable review and I might even look into selling that product because it was a good product that had real value and was marketed accurately and responsibly. In other words, the product is something that I feel would have value to a wide range of people. It is something other people with similar needs should be aware of.

But on the flip-side, if I purchase a piece of crap, I want others to know about that as well. Not so much to trash the seller or affiliate, but to make sure other people do not get cheated as well. Much like I would have appreciated a heads up before I purchased, I like to give others a head up when I get cheated.

I think everyone should do this but they should go about it in the right way. I read reviews on products when I am looking for something on a site like Amazon or similar website. But I often notice that even the best and most respected products have bad reviews and some of those reviews are scathing in their content. I wonder how something can make 100 people very happy but really anger one person all at the same time.

Sometimes I click on the reviewer of a really bad review and I see they have written 50 reviews and all of them are negative and scathing. Now this tells me that this is a very angry person or someone who is very picky or both.

Then I look at the content of some of those reviews and see why it was bad. This can tell you something about the reviewer.

I read the reviews of a new how-to book and it has 47 good reviews and one bad one. The review said "Utterly worthless. A five minute read." That was the entire review. Now that particular book was over 120 pages so I cannot possibly see how that would be called a "5 minute read."

The point I am trying to make is to be objective in your reviews. If you see something bad, write about it. But if there is good, include that as well. And if something is bad, explain why you think it was bad. Maybe your needs are different than someone else's so that same book you hated might be good for them.

In other words, give honest reviews. Don't bring a personal agenda into your reviews. Don't slam a product because you are producing a competing product and want to convince people to purchase yours. It is getting so hard to find accurate and unbiased information these days so please don't make it even harder by posting your own phony or overly negative reviews.

But if you purchased a product and support was really bad, let people know. If the product was not as advertised, let people know that as well. Your information is important because you are the person who actually purchased and used the product. You are the perfect person to educate other people as to what they should or should not purchase.

But the process only works when it is based on honesty and integrity. It does not work well when it is perverted by people pushing their own products and agendas through dishonest or misleading review and comments. This is one way that you can help other make the right decisions just like comments and reviews hopefully help you make your decisions.

How to Protect Yourself & Resolve Problems

At this point we probably have made our decision to purchase and have possibly experienced some kind of negative event. Maybe the product arrived damaged, maybe it wasn't what was advertised and maybe you didn't even get the product at all! Whatever the problem might be, there are right and wrong ways to go about resolving it.

Though this is far from a complete and comprehensive list, here are a few things to consider when handling a problem with an online purchase:

Requesting Refunds

The first thing you should do whenever you are not satisfied is to nicely request a refund. Almost every web-based product will have a guarantee on their webpage. Follow the reporting process and nicely request a refund.

Do NOT be annoying or confrontational when requesting your refund. It is one thing to say "I regret that this product is not what I expected and I would like a refund according to your 30 day money back guarantee. Thank you." It is something else entirely to say "Your friggin' product is a steaming pile of crap. Give me my damned money back or else." This is very true when it comes to your first attempt at getting the refund.

This step is required because most claims or consumer services expect you to go to the manufacturer or the seller first and try to resolve things through proper channels. If you have not tried that already they will tell you to do that first and then come back to them if the matter is still unresolved. So do yourself a favor and save yourself some time by going to the seller or manufacturer first and requesting a refund.

Credit Cards vs. PayPal vs. Money Orders

Whenever you have any kind of dispute, you might feel powerless in trying to fight an entire company by yourself without any kind of leverage.

After all, you are just one customer against the entire company and if they refuse your request, you might not have any other recourse.

That's why all online purchases should be made using either a credit card or PayPal. Between the two, I would choose the credit card. While PayPal might be easier, I honestly believe you have more protection with a major credit card.

Here's why:

If you have a problem with a company and they will not resolve your problem, all you can do is threaten not to do business with them anymore. What that means to them is that they lose your $50 or maybe $100 purchase. Big deal. They can afford to lose you as a customer. They will just replace you.

But if the credit card company demands that they refund the purchase and they tell them no, the credit card company can tell them they cannot accept credit cards anymore for online purchases!

That essentially means they are out of business because an online merchant that doesn't accept credit cards will soon be out of business! So you now have a ton more "clout" or influence when it comes through your credit card company.

To make things even better for you, the credit card comp any can do the refund on their own and just debit the sellers account! So you get your refund and you leave it up to the seller and the credit card company to fight it out between them! All you care about is getting your refund so it works for you!

Sales made through PayPal operate pretty much the same way but PayPal has a dispute resolution process you need to go through online. They give the seller a change to respond and if that doesn't work PayPal will intercede and try to mediate a resolution.

This is better for you than going it alone against the company but I have had a few disputes where PayPal has sided with the seller or they said certain ambiguous deadline had passed and the dispute was denied.

Granted this was a few years ago and their policies and processes may have changed over the years, but I still prefer credit cards. This is not a knock on PayPal it is just my personal opinion. I still use PayPal for most of my online purchases.

Independents vs. Large Retailers

If given a choice I almost always buy from larger or more established sellers or retailer when it comes to online purchases. If I find that I am purchasing through an affiliate link, I feel more confident and comfortable when I have to go through one of the major affiliate networks such as Clickbank or JVZoo. At least with larger retailers and networks they have their own reputation to protect so they will want to mediate and resolve disputes to help keep their reputation intact.

Smaller retailer can mean anything from an unknown store in another state to someone working out of their bedroom closet. This also can include the guy setting up a bogus storefront and then taking it down after it becomes a known scam site. Once the website is down and you can't contact them, unless the sale went through PayPal you might be out of luck.

Even if you did purchase through PayPal if the seller cleaned out his or her PayPal account and then took off, you might still be out of luck.

Generally speaking the larger the retailer the more concerned they are with their reputation and the more they will take action to keep that reputation intact. Your refund is a small matter compared to the damage that could be done to their reputation. So you have a much better chance of getting satisfaction than you would from a scammer operating out of their bedroom closet!

Screenshots & Records

If you find out that something you purchased was a scam or that you were cheated in any way, the first thing you should do is go to the website where you purchased the product and do a screen shot so you can print out the webpage.

This will give you a record to show how the product was marketed, what claims were made and other important information you can use in your complaint.

Without proof you might be faced with a situation where you say one thing and the seller says another. If you have a screen shot of the webpage, you have proof. If you do take a screen shot or print out the page, make sure the web address is in the copy or picture so there is proof of what actual page you went to.

Do this quickly before the website owner takes the page down. This will often happen when the owner knows complaints are rolling in and that he might be in trouble. So get the page printed as soon as you can. Sometimes if the seller knows you have a printed version of their old sales page that might be enough for them to just give in and issue you a refund. They will do this because it is no longer their word against your because you have proof!

Also, keep copies of receipts and all correspondence you have had regarding this problem. If phone calls were made keep a record of when the call was and who you spoke to with a summary of what was said and how the call was left off. Be as detailed and descriptive as possible.

WHOIS

Sometimes there is no contact information whatsoever on the website. So if you have a problem, you have nowhere to turn. If that is the case, you can do a WHOIS search and that might tell you the name and address and e-mail of the website owner. Unless the owner has paid a fee to have this information blocked you can get a contact easily and free of charge just by checking and doing a WHOIS search.

Post Office

If you purchased a physical product that was delivered to you or you responded to an advertisement that came to you through the mail then you can contact the Postmaster in your local Post Office and report the problem to them. They might be able to file a complaint or at least go after them if several complaints have been received about that same business or individual. It might not help you get your money back but it might help save someone else the same problem that you are having right now.

Consumer Affairs

Every state and most local governments have some form of Consumer Affairs Agency designed to help and protect consumers. If you have a problem you cannot resolve or if you have been cheated or scammed, report it to your local Consumer Affairs office. Sometimes just a letter from them is all it takes to get that refund check delivered to your mailbox!

In most states this might be called the Consumer Protection Agency.

Attorney General

If things really get ugly or frustrating, your States Attorney Office may be able to help. They get involved in criminal prosecution of scammers and people who cheat the public. If several complaints about a business or person are received by their office they might start an investigation. But use this option only when all other methods have produced no results.

One drawback to this method is that you usually have to contact the States Attorney in the state where the business is being operated. So you will need to find that out before you know who to notify. Sometimes this is a lot easier said than done.

Other Options for Reporting Online Fraud or Scams:

Federal Trade Commission:
http://www.ftccomplaintassistant.gov

Internet Crime Complaint Center:
http://www.ic3.gov.complaint

Filing Consumer Complaints:
http://www.usa.gov

Better Business Bureau:
http://www.bbb.org

StopFraud.gov
http://stopfraud.gov/report.html

Conclusion

I should say right off the bat that the vast majority of sites on the internet are good site and are full of relevant information. I am sure some of you reading this book now feel the whoever wrote this book is a paranoid and angry person who doesn't trust anyone and who always feels like someone is out to screw them.

I honestly would not feel that way because things have changed in this world and we can no longer live every day giving everyone the benefit of the doubt and blindly trusting everyone we meet and everything we see and hear. It certainly is not the way I would prefer to go through life but it is now the world we live in and we must learn to adapt in order to survive.

What I am advocating is not a level of paranoia but instead a healthy level of questioning everything in life. We should never take anything at face value. We should be inquisitive and challenge things that either do not make sense to us or things that appear to be false or misleading. This is what we should be conditioned to do.

In fact, scammers and people out to cheat us do not want us to ask questions and they do not want us to seek out information or become smarter and more aware. They would greatly prefer us to remain blissfully unaware and trusting because that is the atmosphere in which they flourish. In their world an educated consumer is their worst enemy!

Part of the reason that I wrote this book is not because I think it will change the world or stop crime and fraud in its tracks. The reason I wrote it was to help raise the awareness of what is going on with advertising and some of the forms of marketing that we are subjected to today.

I know the mindset of marketers because when I wanted to learn how to market my products online I attended webinars and conference call where all these techniques were described and how they almost forced people to purchase products and services without fully thinking the purchase all the way through.

I ended most of these "training sessions" feeling like I needed a shower. It just felt wrong and I didn't like it. I think the worst part was the realization one day that it was not one or two marketers that taught these strategies or approaches but rather most of them that listened to. I also realized that they taught these approaches because they worked. They talked about them because they sold a lot of product.

I realized they worked because people were blissfully unaware of what was going on around them when it came to what they read or heard. They were being manipulated without even realizing what was going on! I wanted to change that by making people aware of these things and making it possible for them to become aware of those things when they see them.

My thought was maybe, just maybe, if these practices no longer produced such great results that somehow marketing and advertising might become just a tiny bit more honest and the internet become more of a place to get meaningful information instead of endless sales pitches.

I have no hidden agenda here and no delusions that his book is somehow going to change marketing attitudes of those who use these techniques and approaches. Neither do I expect anyone to abandon things that work well for them just because one guy doesn't think they are right.

But I do believe that if more people become aware, and more people spread the word, that we can change things. After all, that is how change happens. It starts with one or two people and then it grows until change is not just requested, change is demanded.

I have done my best to be totally honest with you throughout this book. I probably made a few people, especially marketers who read this book, angry and a few people probably look at this book after finishing it and wonder what my "angle" was in writing it.

If you are one of those who is trying to figure out my "angle" than I am more than pleased because now at least you are looking at things differently and starting to question things. In that regard this book and my efforts have paid dividends.

But in full disclosure I can honestly tell you I have no agenda. There were no product links or affiliate links contained in this book. I'm promoting anything in this book and I have mentioned no products anywhere within this book either. No commissions will be generated by anything in this book. It is totally agenda free.

While this book will be found on sale in one of the largest online sales outlets, it is not going to make me a fortune. The price will be at most a couple of dollars and some of you who catch it upon its release will get your copy for less and maybe even free. Even when you pay the couple of dollars the publishing fees will eat up a decent chunk of that anyway so I am not about to retire early or anything like that from this book.

At this point I wish you luck and hope that what you learned on these pages has made you a more ware and careful shopper. If not, please go back to the beginning and red this book again!

A Note to My Readers

I hope you have enjoyed this book and have received some real value from reading it. I have tried my best to make it enjoyable and useful reading and hope that you found reading it a good use of your time.

I would like to ask a favor of you. Please recommend this book to your friends and if possible, go to Amazon.com and leave a review so others might see how useful this book can be to them. I would like as many people as possible to see this book and learn from it.

If you would like to learn more about advertising and honest reviews and commentary, you can visit this website:

http://www.honestandethicalreviews.com

It's one place you can go without getting scammed or mislead.

www.ingramcontent.com/pod-product-compliance
Lightning Source LLC
Chambersburg PA
CBHW070539290526
45790CB00002B/564